SOUL SAVING
STORIES

SOUL SAVING STORIES

By

JOHN POWERS

PAULIST PRESS
New York/Mahwah, N.J.

The publisher gratefully acknowledges use of the following material: excerpts from *The Christian Community Bible: Catholic Pastoral Edition*, co-published by Claretian Publications, Quezon City, Philippines and St. Paul Publications, Makati, Philippines; the *Crossmaker* character was originally published in an earlier version of *If They Could Speak: Ten Witnesses to the Passion*, published by Twenty-Third Publications, Mystic, Connecticut.

Cover design by Calvin Chu
Book design by Cynthia Dunne

LIBRARY OF CONGRESS CATALOGING-IN PUBLICATION DATA

Powers, John, 1949–
Soul saving stories / by John Powers.
p. cm.
ISBN 0-8091-3730-5 (alk. paper)
1. Bible stories, English—N.T. Gospels. 2. Bible N.T.—History of Biblical events—Fiction. I. Title
BS550. 2. P686 1997
225. 9'505—dc21   97-14703
                                                         CIP

Published by Paulist Press
997 Macarthur Blvd.
Mahwah, New Jersey 07430

❧

I dedicate this book of characters
to my Brothers and Sisters:
Tom, Peter, Mary, Ann, Margaret and Kathleen.

❧

My thanks also to those who have helped restore me
to sanity and restory me to serenity,

Jeff Anderson, Susan Boyle Busque, Eugene Bonacci,
Nick Bonadies, Mark Dupont, Daniel Eakin,
Brice Edwards, Michael Foley, Graig Harrison, Robert Joerger,
Terence Kristofak, Michael Nelson, Bill Perri, Tom Pollard,
Francis Roberge, Kevin Sousa, Bill Walsh,
the members of the Passionist Community and the staff
of St. Michael's Paraclete Community.

❧

CONTENTS

INTRODUCTION

"If citizens of the bible could speak to us today, what might they say?" *Soul Saving Stories* answers this question in a collection of creative scripture soliloquies that are so emotionally moving—so well defined—that the images become forcefully arresting and unforgettable.

In separate midrashed monologues about the common issues of the human story—fear and courage, rejection and acceptance, scapegoating and responsibility, success and failure, truth and denial—I explore how our thinking has not changed over the years despite complicating factors of time, morals, class and culture. The bible characters within these pages are presented in monodramas for the sole/soul purpose of adding a personal dimension to the bible, thus making it relevant to people today.

If you are seeking a greater understanding of humanity, for the *sake* of humanity, I believe these soul saving stories are consistent enough with the original intent of the bible to point us directly to the truth in a sort of unique "self-study" program of spiritual psychotherapy.

Although *Soul Saving Stories* is a work of fiction, the tales told are true.

Fiction can tell the truth as well as fact can, and perhaps, at times, with even fuller meaning. Fiction has imagination on its side—that nation of images, that incredible resource, that energy that helps us to re-story our lives.

Albert Einstein says that "the imagination is more important than knowledge." If this is true, then it is also true that revelation cannot exist without imagination.

Kathleen R. Fischer, author of *The Inner Rainbow* (Paulist Press 1983), tells us that only imagination enables us to reach the *heart* of Christian ministry. We must embody imaginative truth in our own persons, she says, so that we can continue Christ's mystery. Thus, we can create an inspiring and uplifting life from an otherwise mundane day-to-day existence.

Soul, the innermost unity of emotion, intuition, mind, body and spirit, is the imagination pointed in the direction of truth.

The most common but also most unjustifiable word linked to the imagination is the word "just." Every time a person says, "It's just your imagination," another possibility dies.

Ann and Barry Ulanov, authors of *The Healing Imagination* (Paulist Press, 1991), tell us that imagination is the creative activity of psyche and soul. This is because it plays in all our ways of being—thinking and feeling, intuiting and sensing. Our psychic life, they tell us, speaks first to us in images before it speaks in words. This combination is always insightful, provocative, and engaging. It provides us with a framework in which we can respond sensibly to our complicated lives.

In *Soul Saving Stories* I will introduce you to some relatively well known and some fairly well unknown bible characters who not only wander in the holy land of scripture but are also alive, well and residing in the collective imagination.

As a parabolist, let me make one very practical suggestion as you read this book of characterizations. *Use* your imagination—don't suspend it. Let your imagination go into the white spaces behind the letters, words and sentences of the bible stories.

Perhaps, then, you will discover that these scripture friends live first in your psyche and soul, in the nation of images that gives you life.

SOUL SAVING STORIES

THE
STORY CARVER

MARK 6 :7-9

Jesus then walked around the village teaching. He summoned the Twelve and began to send them out two by two, giving them authority over evil spirits. And he ordered them to take nothing for the journey except a walking stick; no food, no bag, no money in their belts. They were to wear sandals and were not to take an extra shirt.

THE STORY CARVER

My name is Benjamin.
I'm the son of a carpenter from Jerusalem.
I'm a woodcarver.
Have been most of my life.
Picked up the trade from my father.

For years I worked side by side with my father
in the carpenter's shed
outside our home
near Golgatha hill.

Loved every minute of his company,
especially when he'd tell me stories.

As my father often said,
"Human beings are storytellers by nature
and, at best,
are nurtured by the traumas and joys of life
to value and share their stories."

I think
I learned more about life from my father's stories
than I ever learned from him about carpentry.

Oh,
I'm not a poor carpenter.
I learned what I needed to make a living.

But, to make a life,
well,
I'd rather listen to and tell stories any day.

As far as I'm concerned,
there's no greater pleasure,
or more intimate human endeavor
than telling someone the tale of your life
or listening to someone else spin his or her story.

After all,

don't we carve our very souls
out of the tragedy, comedy, irony and romance
of our lives?

Sharing our stories is soul-making.

If human time is anything,
it is a storied affair.

In a very real way
stories are us.

In fact,
I believe
that where two or three are gathered together
honestly sharing their stories
there is God in their midst.

Well,
since a story is really a community of memories
let me tell you one about my father and me.

"Papa," I said as we worked in the shop,
"tell me the story you told me yesterday."

"But, you already know that story,"
my father replied.
"Why do you want to hear it again?"
he asked.

"Oh, but Papa," I answered,
"it's your favorite story in the whole world
and you love telling it so much.
Tell it to me again, please?"

With that
my father put down his tools,
sat down,
smiled slightly
and said,

"On the sixth day,
after the God who is nameless

had created the mountains and oceans,
light and darkness,
the birds of the air,
the fish of the sea,
and animals of all kinds,
God decided to play in the mud
on the banks of the river
that God had scratched into the earth
with a walking stick.

"God played almost all day in the mud,
forming, shaping and reshaping the wet humus, soil,
into the first animal to become human.

"God had designed many other animals,
with legs going this way,
arms going that,
brains the size of peas or plums,
tails to follow up the rear
and heads that could turn almost all the way around,
but God had a unique design in mind
for the being that would become human.

"The legs God stretched long enough
to lean uphill or down.

"The head God put on the top
to be closer to the sky.

"The eyes God made big enough
to see far and wide in the light
but only a short distance in the dark.

"The heart God put in the middle
with a beat and rhythm to keep pace too.

"The brain God made just the right size
for imagining, knowing and feeling.

"God made every organ of the body out of the wet earth,
molding each with a fine beauty and function
all its own.

"God then wove into the marrow of the bones,
fiber of muscle
and core of the brain
the instincts of an animal
without which the mud
could never become fully human.

"Then God
poked a big divine finger into the muddy face
to form a mouth
just round enough,
and with a tongue just pointed enough,
to make words and tell stories.

"Finally,
God took two divine fingers
and, gently placing one
on each side of the human's head,
scratched out openings
large enough for hearing.

"God played for hours
fashioning just the right design for the ears.

"It was delicate work,
shaping the precise curves
to catch the nuance and meaning of sound.

"When God had finally finished forming the first human
God leaned on a mighty, thick walking stick,
knelt down in the brown river,
bent over,
put divine lips to muddy lips,
and breathed the spirit of life
into the first being to become human.

"When God had breathed just enough spirited life
into the human
to last for an eternity of change,
God's lips moved just a few inches,
to the ear of the muddy being,

and whispered,
'Once upon a time.'

"And with that,
the human coughed and gasped,
took the deepest of deep breaths,
huuuuuuuuuuuuuuu,
and the story came to life.

"The nameless one
simply leaned heavily on the divine walking stick,
sat back in the water,
rested from a day of play
and listened."

Of course,
when I was young
I couldn't do the intricate woodwork my father did
or carve a truthful tale as he did so smoothly.

Eventually, though,
I learned the craft
of carving a good story out of lived life.

I'll never forget my father at the bench,
hewing fine tables for someone's home
or chiseling strong tools for a field worker.

My father, even for a time,
sad to say,
was forced to cut the rough crossbeams
used for crucifixion by the Roman terrorists.

Of course,
my father would never allow me
to help with the carving of the crossbeams.

"No son of mine," he'd say,
"is going to be forced into working for violence."

If someone had to do the crude work
of chiseling crosses

to protect and feed the family,
it would be my father.

My task,
when first apprenticed with my father
was to carve simple walking sticks
for the travelers
who made their way in and out of the city.

It was big business.
Demand was always higher than supply.

A traveler wouldn't think of leaving the city
for the road
without a good strong walking stick
to guide, support, protect
and companion him along the way.

So, here I still sit,
on the edge of the city,
in view of Golgatha hill,
carving walking sticks
and trading stories
with travelers who dare the way of the road.

Oh,
you don't have to be rich
to purchase one of my walking sticks.

In fact,
for a poor traveler
I often make an even swap.

You tell me your story,
where you've been and where you're going,
and I'll give you one of my story-sticks.

That's what I've come to call
my carved walking sticks.
Story-sticks.
Think about it.
Isn't a story just like a walking stick?

Both stories and sticks
guide us on the road,
especially through the tangles and thorns,
support us when the road gets rough,
protect and save us
from human and not so human dangers,
and in truth
are like companions that faithfully keep company.

I actually believe
that a good story-stick
can help you get from here
to the only important "there" there is.

After all,
isn't that what most travelers want to do,
get from "here" to "there"?

For example,
I met a man once upon a time
who desperately sought after,
fantasized about and wished for only one thing,
to get out of "here" and to get to,
where else,
but the happily ever after of "there."

The traveler hated "here."

"Here," he felt
sad, bored, lonely, frustrated, angry,
afraid, poor, ugly, empty and in the dark.

"Who wouldn't want to get away from 'here,'"
he cried.

"'Here' is for losers.
'There' is for winners.
'There' is
greener, warmer, more comfortable,
peaceful, beautiful and brighter
than 'here' could ever be."

The traveler took every easy road
that stretched before him
to get from "here" to "there."

He tried the escape routes of
fantasy, denial, addiction, greed, prestige,
power, position, depression, and fundamentalist religion,
and on and on he traveled
down this seemingly smooth road
and that so-called easy path
to get to his desperately desired "there."

The faster he sped,
however,
to get from "here" to "there,"
the further "there" seemed to be from "here."

Finally,
frustrated that he was not able
on his own
to get out of "here" and get "there,"
he resigned himself to being,
of all places, "here."

Slowly, so slowly
it almost seemed as if he was going backward
over all the trails he'd traveled,
sad resignation
turned into a bit of heartfelt acceptance.

Eventually,
when the traveler fell headlong into muddle age
—not middle age but muddle age—
he realized he needed to ask for help.

That's when the traveler arrived at my shop,
seeking directions and a walking stick.

"I can certainly carve you a fine story-stick,"
I answered to his request,
"but regarding directions from 'here' to 'there,'

well,
I can't help you 'there.'

I have an idea, though,"
I said.

"Perhaps
if we tell each other
which roads we've each already taken,
that took us nowhere fast,
we might discover the untried path."

So,
while I carved the traveler's story-stick
we shared our tales of the road,
how we'd each gotten lost along the way,
to the so-called
happily-ever-after
of "there."

When, at last,
we fell into a long silence,
I gave the traveler his new story-stick,
and off he went,
carrying firmly in his grip
the lessons life's story has to teach us all:

that there never was a "there" there anyway,
that "there" is actually already "here,"

that no matter where you go
you can't get away from "here,"

that "here" is found in every "there,"

and that all you have to add to "here"
to find yourself "there"
is a graceful touch of acceptance.

After all,
the only once-upon-a-time
or happily-ever-after

you'll ever find
is already "here."

Stories help you learn the way to "here."

It's a wise traveler
who accepts the support
of a good strong story-stick
along the way.

Stories carry energy, truth, lessons, insight, emotions.

At least
that's what I try to cut into every story-stick I carve.

So,
my friends,
take up your stories and follow me,
as I show you how best to walk with a story-stick.

The road can be pretty rough,
and very long.

In fact,
I've been told by a lifelong traveler
that you can expect to walk almost 115,000 miles
in your average life.

So,
let's practice the art of walking.
Practice may make for a bit of progress.

When walking
you have to lean forward slightly,
lose your balance just a bit,
and begin to fall.

To walk
you must constantly let go of the previous stability,
falling all the time,
trusting that you will find
a succession of new stabilities
with each step.

Walking, however,
can be risky business
especially when climbing a steep grade
or gingerly making your way down into the valley.

Falling is a risk you take with every step.

The story-stick is here
to help you keep your balance
or to help you rise up when you stumble and fall.

If you take the risk to lean on your own story
it will support you for another step,
and then another,
and then another.

If you carry your own tried and true story-stick
you'll also be protected
and perhaps even saved
from the dangers of the road.
That's right,
I believe stories have the power to save us,
especially from ourselves.

Here's a fable about another traveler
you might consider.

I carved a story-stick
in exchange for this tale.

The traveler was walking through the great forest
of trees and buildings
when he came upon a snake
sunning himself in the middle of the path.

Frightened by the snake he saw
the traveler picked up the closest stick he could find
to kill the snake.

The problem was,
however,
that the snake he saw was really a stick

and the stick he picked up
was really a snake.

After asking the traveler to repeat his twisted tale
(that the snake he saw was really a stick
and the stick he picked up was really a snake)
I asked the man a few probing questions.

First, I asked
what he feared most in life,
what terrified him along the way.

"Well,"
he answered with head down,
"I'm most afraid of what others might think of me
if they knew what a mistake-making fool I can be."

"Ah," I answered,
"so the fear of what others will think of you
is the snake waiting for you on the path.

"What stick, then,
did you pick up
to kill such a slithering fear?"
I asked.

"Well,"
he answered while blushing,
"I usually keep my story to myself.
In fact,
I prefer to travel alone.
You never know whom you can trust along the way."

"So," I said,
"the stick you picked up
to kill the frightening snake
of what others might think of you
was actually the more poisonous serpent
of isolation and mistrust.

"Certainly a more deadly enemy
than the judgment of others

could ever be,
don't you think?"

Perhaps
the greatest truth I've learned
from many travelers
who have purchased my carved story-sticks
has been that the road is always safer
and much more enjoyable
when you travel two by two.

Let me at this point
make a few suggestions
regarding traveling companions.

I recommend that you:

—walk only with those who can admit
that they belong to the community of the
used, abused and confused.

They're much better company.

—take the risk
of putting your story-stick out in front
to meet the road first,
whether others trust you
with their tale of travels or not.

Perhaps
they're just more afraid
of what you will think of them
than you are
of what they will think of you.

—listen carefully, however,
to any companions courageous enough
to share their life tale with you.

Such sharing can become fuel for the road.

—never change directions
just because a larger group

is hurriedly going another way.

Don't let others tell you what path to take
or what your story should be.

Follow the authority of your own true experience,
not just the experience of someone else's authority.

—avoid those who need to say
"been there" or "done that."

You can be pretty sure neither is true.

—travel only with those
content to be followers of the way,
rather than with those
with enough contempt to want always to lead the way.

—remember, when you come to mountains or valleys,
that no one said
you have to keep pace with your companions.

After all,
everyone needs a little down time.

—and, finally,
walk only with those searching for truth.

You know,
I've met the truth.
He's a tall order.
He was on the road.

Actually,
the first time I saw the truth
I avoided him.

He was stark naked.

I felt embarrassed
that the truth was so exposed and raw.

Down the road,
however,

I ran into the truth again.

This time,
he was dressed in the finest of parables and fables
and walking with a fine story-stick.

Of course,
I know no parable can cover the whole truth.

Still,
wrapped in parables,
the truth can be a pleasure to behold.

Now,
I've been a carver of stories almost all my life,
a storyteller,

a maggid or misapear in Hebrew,
le conteur in French,
el cuentista in Spanish,
Rozpravac in Slovak
Bajarz in Polish,
Novelliere Narratore in Italian,
Ananse Seem in Akan, African dialect,
Badmapan in Armenian,
Kiventista in Tagalog, Philippino dialect,
Mythologos in Greek,
Narrator in Latin,
Sean chai in Gaelic,
Xing Giu Shi do Jen in Chinese,

a teller of tales,
a spinner of yarns,
a midrash maker,
a weaver of narrativity.

I've carved hundreds,
perhaps thousands of story-sticks,
to help travelers on their way.

I've carved story-sticks for the great,
near great,

greatly poor
and those who just grate me the wrong way.

Why,
I even carved a story-stick
for one of the greatest Parabolists in history,
the rebbe Jesus of Nazareth.

It was only a few days before Passover when Jesus,
and one of his followers,
Mark by name,
I think,
came into my little shop near Golgatha hill.

After telling me
that he too was the son of a carpenter
and had carved many a story-stick in his day
he asked
to purchase one of my poorly fashioned sticks.

"Oh no, rebbe," I said.
"You are renowned throughout the land
as one who shares
the most telling of tales
and saving stories.

I will trade you any stick you see in my shop
for just one word of revelation."

Jesus then picked up
one of the most knotted and twisted of sticks
and said,

"In the beginning was not only the word,
but the phrase, sentence, paragraph,
chapter and Story,
and the Story was with God.
And the Story was God;
the Story was in the beginning with God."

Only days later
I found the same twisted story-stick

that Jesus had carried away from my shop,
leaning,
balanced against a heavy boulder,
just outside an empty tomb
near Golgatha hill.

An empty tomb.

Now there's a story
that will last,
at least as long as,
say,
forever.

THE TREASURE SEEKER

MATTHEW 13:44

*The kingdom of heaven
is like a treasure
hidden in a field.*

*The man who finds it
buries it again;
and so happy is he,
that he goes and sells everything he has,
so that he can buy the field.*

THE TREASURE SEEKER

Did you know
that most of the stories Jesus told
were true?

Well,
I'm not positive
that all the tales he told
actually happened.

As a matter of fact,
now that I think about it,
I can vouch
only for the authenticity
of the stories
I told Jesus,
as we worked together in the fields.

You see,
I knew Jesus and his parents quite well
since my father's farm
was just outside the village of Nazareth.

In fact,
whenever my father needed good carpentry work
he'd call on Joseph,
certainly the most talented carpenter
in the area.

It's too bad
that Jesus never picked up
his father's ability
to work with wood though,
so when Joseph died
Jesus had to find
whatever work he could.

Since I knew,
however,

what it was like to lose a father,
I decided to hire Jesus
to work in my fields
clearing rocks.

The work,
I hoped,
would not only help Jesus support his mother
but would give him something to do
as he grieved his terrible loss.

Besides, anyone who would argue with the old men
in the temple
I wanted working for me.

Every rock
that stood in the way of the plow
became a personal challenge
for the young man.

He was a good worker
and an even better companion,
especially when we'd take a break from our work
to rest and talk.

I'll never forget,
for example,
one particularly blistering hot day
as Jesus and I
took a few minutes' refuge from the open field
to sit in the shade of an olive grove.

We sat silently for a time
just looking out over the half-plowed field,
when Jesus finally spoke up,
saying:

"A rich piece of land is like a treasure."

"That's almost
exactly what my father used to tell my older brother and me
when we were children,"

I said.

Suddenly,
I could almost see my father
standing out in the middle of the field,
with his rough hands at the plow,
turning to my brother and me,
as we picked rocks out of the overturned earth,
and saying,
"Boys,
there's a treasure buried in this field,
a treasure that will be yours someday."

Of course,
when I was young
I believed my father's treasure tales
so much that I dreamed of one day digging it up.

As I grew older,
however,
my father seemed to grow crazier.

My brother and I
usually just laughed behind his back
as he rambled on about the treasure,
the treasure.

If there was such a treasure
why hadn't he dug it up,
the old fool?
At least that way
he could live in ease and comfort
instead of all of us having to break our backs
laboring in the fields.

When my father
would hear my brother and me
snickering at
his tall treasure tales
he'd quietly remark again,
"The treasure is your inheritance."

My father was a wise man.
I know that now.
I'm just sorry
I didn't know it when I was younger.

I guess
I just wasn't
ready to put my hands to the plow.

In fact,
it wasn't
until after my father died
that I really learned
to appreciate his wisdom.

You see,
when I was young
I was a bit arrogant,
rather self-centered to be honest about it.

So much so
that I was able
to convince my father
to sell one of his fields
so that
I could take my share of the inheritance
and go on my way.

I had no intention
of spending the rest of my life
breaking my back plowing and planting,
so I begged, demanded,
and manipulated my father
into selling the field
and splitting the money
between my brother and me.

With the money finally in hand
I left home
in search of the easy life.

Can you believe
I actually thought
the world owed me a living,
that the riches of comfort and security
were mine for the taking?

It wasn't,
however,
until I returned home,
after years of aimless living,
that I finally realized
that my father
was right all along.

There really is a treasure
buried in the field of life.

Oh,
it isn't a box of silver or gold
that makes life easy.

It's something far more precious.

Hidden in the field of every person's life is a treasure,
a treasure of truth,
the kind that sets you free
with purpose and meaning.

I had to learn this truth the hard way,
but
you know what they say;
"Hard lessons can be the best learned."

Ultimately
I learned the lessons life had to teach,
because I was lucky enough to find
—or was it they who found me,
who knows?—
anyway I had some great teachers along the way,
mentors willing
to share their treasure of truth with me.

I remember,
for example,
a Samaritan man
who taught me
what real compassion is.

You see, after I left home
with my share of the money
from the sale of my father's field,
I wandered aimlessly,
spending my money wildly.

Eventually,
my travels
put me on the Jericho road
where I was unlucky enough
to run into a band of thieves.

Of course,
when I refused
to turn my money over to the bandits
they simply beat it from me,
leaving me half dead
on the side of the road.

As I lay dying
in that dirty ditch,
all the stupidity and arrogance of my life
flashed before my eyes.

I have never felt
as lonely and helpless as at that moment,
especially as I watched
two so-called charitable types,
a priest and a Levite,
pause momentarily
to shake their heads in disgust
and then stroll on.

Finally,
someone did stop to help,

however,
much to my surprise.

It was a Samaritan,
a man who was
by custom
supposed to keep his distance from a Jew.

I'll never forget this man's goodness
as he bandaged my wounds,
carried me to an inn
and paid the innkeeper
to take care of me
as long as necessary.

I never in my wildest dreams
imagined that there actually were
people as compassionate as this Samaritan was.

It made no sense
that someone should go
so far out of his way for me.

When
I eventually tried to thank the man for his kindness
he said something
that has become a treasure of truth for me.

He simply shrugged his shoulders
and said,
"I give as I receive."

As far as I was concerned
this Samaritan was God's compassionate hand,
and all he would say was,
"I give as I receive."

The Samaritan
wasn't the only teacher
to share a treasure of truth with me,
however.

There's another mentor

I'll never forget,
not only for the truth he taught me
but also because
he smelled worse than any person I've ever met.

This old man was a pig-feeder.

He managed the feeding of hundreds of pigs
on the farm
where I got a job
after I recovered from the robbery and beating.

Remarkably
it was on that pig farm
that a great truth was revealed:

The truth that
in the final analysis
there are no easy roads,
only those you pave with your own choices.

You have to make the roads you travel.
You have to make your own life.

You may not believe it,
or—who knows?—maybe you will:
I was a terrible pig-slopper,
the worst.

At least
that's what the old pig-feeder told me
when he finally fired me.

After telling me
that not even the pigs liked me very much,
he said,
"For God's sake, boy,
and your own,
go home.

"Go home
and find out where your heart belongs.

"It's obvious,"
he said,
"that your treasure
isn't hidden in the mud of the pigpens,
so go home."

I understood
immediately what the pig-feeder meant.

I knew
he didn't mean
that I should move back into my father's house
just to have
the security of four walls.

No,
the home the pig-feeder wanted me to return to
was the home within myself.

From the pig-feeder
I learned that you have to
dig for the treasure of truth in your own backyard,
in your own life.

You have to belong to yourself
before you can belong anywhere else.

So, with guilt and shame
as my companions,
I made my way home
to find my truth.

Did you ever notice, my friends,
that the road that returns you home
almost always seems
shorter than the road that takes you away?

It certainly seemed that way to me,
because
within only days of my decision
to return home
I turned the last bend
on the road to my father's house,

there to find my father
standing firmly in the middle of the path,
as though he'd anticipated my return.

Now,
either my father knew I was coming home that day
or he came out to wait for me every day.

Either way,
I finally realized
as I walked that final stretch of road
that my father loved me the best way he knew how,
by waiting for me to return his love.

I'll never forget
as I stepped shamefully up to my father
to beg for forgiveness
how firmly he took my neck in his hands
and how he kissed me.

He refused to let me bow my head in humiliation,
wanting me instead
to meet him eye to eye.

When I tried to tell him how sorry I was
for ignoring his love,
he responded
by embracing me again.

Where I'd traveled
and what I'd done
was not as important
to my father
as the fact
that I'd come home
to dig for the treasure of truth
in my own back yard.

It seems
that there's no greater fulfillment for parents
than to see their children
find the treasure of happiness.

This was certainly true for my father
because no one
enjoyed himself more
at the party he gave upon my return
than he did.

Why,
he was even able
to love my resentful older brother
into letting go of his anger
to join in the celebration.

Now,
please don't misunderstand me here.

I'm not proud of what I did,
taking my father's hard-earned money
and throwing it away on meaningless pleasures,
but I learned through the pain of it all.

I don't recommend
that anyone seek out the teacher pain,
but I have to admit that
pain was a mentor
that pointed the way home for me.

Once home,
however,
I had a great deal of work to do.

I had to purchase back
the field my father sold
to give me my share of the inheritance.

After my brother and I
healed the wounds of our anger,
nothing could stop us
from doing everything we could
to buy back the field of treasure.

It took us years,
selling all that we had,

working wherever we could
to get enough money
to purchase that field.

Of course,
once we settled the field's ownership,
we had even more work to do.

We had to dig for the treasure
my father had promised
was buried in our own back yard.

Every day
we'd go out to dig.

For two solid years
all my brother and I did
was dig hole after hole
looking for the treasure.

It was damn frustrating work.
Every hole we dug was empty.

If there was a treasure in the field
as my father promised,
where the hell was it,
we wondered?

When we asked my father
to tell us exactly where he buried the treasure
all he'd say was,
"You have to plow it up yourself."

Finally,
frustrated by not finding the treasure
and since
we had no other income at the time,
my brother and I decided
that we might as well
plant some seed
in the already-turned-over earth.

Pretty soon,
of course,
we had a small harvest to cut,
which took us away from our treasure hunt.

Since the harvest that year was small
we decided
to plow and plant a bit more the next.

As the years went on
we plowed and planted more and more of the field
until there was no more time or desire
to look for the treasure
my father promised was buried there.

Gradually,
gradually
after years
of digging, plowing, planting and harvesting,
I finally realized
where my father's treasure of inheritance
really was hidden—
in the living of life itself.

I understood then
that the treasure of life
can't be merely dug up.

If you seek the truth
you have to plant the seeds of faith and hope.

If you want to find life's treasure
you have to work your own life
to bring in the harvest of meaning.

Let me share with you
the real treasures
I've discovered
by working the field
in my own back yard,
the lessons that life has taught me.

First,
I've learned
that you can't plow someone else's field
to find your truth.

If you don't plow and plant your own field
you can't find the treasure
of belonging, of home, of heart.

I've learned
that no one
is going to move the rocks and boulders out of your way
either.

Either you find the strength to move them yourself,
live around them
or ask for help.

These are your only options.

The healthiest,
of course,
is to ask for help.

I've learned
that everyone has a field to plow
and that
I am obligated
to do what I can
to help those
who either do not have a mule
to pull their plowshare
or to help those
whose plows have been bent by the boulders.

I've learned that it's always good
to stop plowing
to make friends
with those who pass by.

Some of the greatest treasures
in my life

have been the people
who have simply wandered into my field.

I've learned
that no one plows through life alone.

I've learned that there's a divine farmer
giving me strength when I'm tired
and purpose when I'm confused.

I've learned
that the field I plow
stretches far beyond this life
into an eternal field,
that once you put your hands and heart to the plow
you can never turn back.

I guess
you're never quite finished your labor
in this life or the next,
so you might as well enjoy the work.

And finally
I've learned that
it's much healthier
to laugh
when I foolishly get my plow stuck in the mud
or when I plow a crooked furrow.

Anyway
these were the lessons I learned
and the stories I told Jesus
as we sat resting in the shade of the olive grove
that afternoon
many years ago.

I must admit,
of course,
that when I finished spinning my tales
I expected Jesus

to say something profound and inspiring
in response.

Jesus,
however,
simply climbed to his feet,
put his hand out to help me up,
and said,
"For God's sake,
and your own,
are you ready to get back to work?"

THE
OUTCAST

LUKE 17:11-17

On the way to Jerusalem,
Jesus was passing along
the border between Samaria and Galilee and,
as he entered a village,
ten lepers came to meet him.

Keeping their distance,
they called to him, "Jesus, Master, have pity on us!"

Then Jesus said to them,
"Go and show yourselves to the priests."

Now, as they went their way,
they found they were cured.

One of them, as soon as he saw he was cleansed,
turned back praising God in a loud voice and,
throwing himself on his face before Jesus,
he gave him thanks.

This man was a Samaritan.

Then Jesus said, "Were not all ten healed?
Where are the other nine?
Was no one found to return and give praise to God
but this alien?"

And Jesus said to him,
"Rise and go your way; your faith has saved you."

THE OUTCAST

I hated
the self-righteous masters of ritual and money,
the priests.

What right did they have,
after all,
to grasp for equality with God,
parade around wrapped in authority,
declaring people with
this illness, that occupation,
this gender, that color,
this orientation or that religious persuasion,
unclean, alien, outcasts,
to be shunned?

For years I was an angry and bitter man,
suffering not only from a physical disease
but from something even worse,
a victim's mentality.

Because society labeled me a misfit
I judged myself the same,
that I wasn't worthy of belonging,
of life or love.
Who am I? you wonder.

Well, I'm one of them,
one of the different, the excluded,
one of the ten lepers
to meet Jesus along the borders of Samaria and Galilee.

You see,
from my early teen years
I suffered the chronic skin ailment known as sara-at,
an illness that condemned me
to live in hiding and humiliation.

I did not, however,
have leprosy
as you know it.

Hansen's disease,
the leprosy of your day,
didn't appear in my country
until the middle ages.

My illness was curable
and I was determined
to do whatever it took
to rid myself of this disease,
to become socially acceptable again.

"So misfits and untouchables, unite!"
I cried.
"Exiled and excluded, rise up!

"Today we seek the healer,
Jesus,
the one who will take away our illness and pain."

My nine companions and I
didn't have to travel far
to find the miracle worker,
for he and his followers
had camped overnight
just outside our village.

When we found the camp
we hid among the brush and trees,
keeping our distance for a time,
fearing that even Jesus might reject us.

Suddenly,
one of the women of our group
cried out to Jesus
for mercy and compassion.

Moved by this woman's daring
the rest of us joined the chorus,

pleading for Jesus
to do whatever he could to cure us.

When Jesus heard our pleas
he turned quickly toward us,
walked right up to us
and told us to go and show ourselves
to the priests at the temple.

As quickly as he came toward us,
just as quickly did he walk away.

Stunned we looked at one another
in disbelief.

Was this man mad?
we wondered.

Nothing had changed.

No healing had taken place
that we could see.

I looked at my arms
and saw what I always saw,
disease.

I looked at myself
and felt what I always felt,
excluded, ashamed,
like an exile in my own homeland.

The more I felt like a victim
of life and prejudice,
however,
the angrier I became.

I was sick of being sick with shame,
of believing
that there was something wrong with me.

Suddenly,
in the midst of my anger,
I realized that I was healed.

Oh,
not of my chronic skin ailment
but of the more terminal disease
of shame itself.

I realized, then,
that by simply including me,
that by just talking with me,
Jesus
had set free in me a growing confidence,
a feeling of value and worth,
a dignity that was rightfully mine.

As I stood transfixed
in that moment of awareness
I knew that I was free to walk out into the open,
yes, a man with a physical illness
but a complete human being nonetheless,
and one who would no longer
let shame and bigotry,
prejudice and social status,
rule his life.

Suddenly
I felt free enough
to go to the priests of the temple
if only to challenge them
with the simply profound truth
that no one has the right
to cast other human beings aside
because they do not measure up
to the standards of a sick society.

In that holy moment of inclusion,
I chose to live as I am,
not merely as I wished to be.

No longer did I need
life or God
to take away what made me different.

Instead I chose
to find life
in the middle of my struggle.

Suddenly
my nine companions
began to hoot and yell,
jumping up and down
with wild laughter.

They too discovered themselves healed
of the shame they suffered.

Could you believe it?
Could anyone believe it?

My friends were so wildly happy
that they ran off in all directions,
some to their families,
others probably straight to the priests
to challenge the status quo.

With joy
tears flowed from my eyes
as I, however,
ran after Jesus.

When I fell on the ground before him
in humble gratitude
I realized how much my life
had been dominated
by what I thought I lacked
rather than by
the dignity
I had been given by life itself.

My friends,
let me ask you a question.

Have you ever felt like an excluded person?

It's a foolish question,

I know.

If you're a human being
you've wondered
at some time or other
whether you belong.

In fact,
there are probably people
(sitting in this room)
(listening to my voice)
right now
who have felt oppressed
by today's unjust social caste structure—
poor people, women,
the physically or emotionally challenged,
those of diverse ethnic or racial backgrounds,
religious beliefs, educational levels
or sexual orientations.

Well,
my friends,
I come to speak with you today
not only to share the story of how I was healed
of a victim's mentality
but more importantly
I come to beg you,
my friends,
to stretch out your faith to the Healer.

Run
to the one who will set your integrity free,
to the one who will include you
no matter what your diversity or disease.

Seek the Lord on the road of your life.

He walks on the borders of faith and hope,
always ready to include you
in his overwhelming love.

Be as you are, my friends,
whole and free,
not just
in spite of your differences or struggles
but through them.

Be thankful
for the life that is yours,
my friends,
and for the opportunity
to make something of it.

Believe in the Lord,
my friends,
and he will heal you
into believing in yourselves.

THE
SHEPHERD

JOHN 10:1-9

"Truly,
I say to you,
he who does not enter the sheepfold by the gate,
but climbs in some other way,
is a thief and a robber.
But the shepherd of the sheep
enters by the gate.
The keeper opens the gate to him
and the sheep hear his voice;
he calls each of his sheep by name
and leads them out.
When he has brought out all of his own,
he goes before them
and the sheep follow him
for they know his voice.
A stranger they will not follow:
rather they will run away from him
because they don't recognize
a stranger's voice."

Jesus used this comparison,
but they did not understand
what he was saying to them.

So Jesus said,
"Truly,
I say to you,

I am the shepherd of the sheep.
All who came were thieves and robbers,
and the sheep did not hear them.
I am the gate.
Whoever enters through me
will be saved;
he will go in and out
freely and find food."

THE SHEPHERD

The first time I heard the whisperings of God,
well,
let me tell you about it.

I couldn't have been more than twelve years old
the night I helped my cousin and father
herd our family's flock of sheep
down a hillside
outside the village of Bethlehem.

Of course,
while my father led the flock,
telling story after story
so that the sheep could follow the sound of his voice,
I trailed the flock,
keeping the stragglers in line,
heading home to the sheepfold
where we could protect them from the wolves.

Anyway,
just as I finished herding
this one rather rambunctious lamb
back into the fold
a brilliance,

brighter than bright,
shone around me.

I'm not sure where the light came from,
whether from within or without me,
or both,
but there I stood flooded in light,
listening to a whisper as soft as dust,
so soft that I could hear
only a few phrases here and there,
phrases like,
"good news," "joy,"
"savior born in Bethlehem," and "peace on earth."

Well,
since I'd never seen a light so bright
nor heard a whisper so soft,
I did what you'd expect of a twelve year old.
I stood frozen.

That was a long time ago now—
in fact,
so long ago that I'd almost forgotten
how terrified I was
when God first spoke to me.

It wasn't,
however,
to be my last encounter with God.

The next divine whisper
came some fifteen or so years later,
when I was again out with the flock,
preparing,
this time with only my cousin,
to lead the flock home for the night,
when suddenly we realized
that we were missing one of our one hundred sheep.

Well my father
wouldn't allow us to lose even one of his flock,

so I sent my cousin home with the remaining ninety-nine
and I set out after the one stray.

Now, I didn't think I'd have to go very far
or that it would take very long
to find the lost lamb
because sheep have a reputation
for being pretty stupid.

As soon as sheep realize they're lost
they do something really dumb—
they just lie down where they are
and bleat and bleat,
until, of course,
either a shepherd or a wolf appears.

Well,
the stray on this particular night
did just that,
bleated in a way you wouldn't believe,
being, of course,
lucky that I got to him before the prowling wolf.

Anyway,
I picked the sheep up
—heavy for a lamb, I thought—
threw him over my shoulders
and started to trudge home.

If I kept up a good pace
I thought I might even catch up
to my cousin and the flock.

A flock of sheep moves rather slowly,
you know,
until, of course,
they pick up the home scent
and then they can really move
if they're of a mind to do so.

I guess that's true of people too,
that the closer you get to your destination

the faster you tend to move toward it.

Well, anyway,
I walked with that sheep flung over my shoulder
for what seemed forever,
but I never did reach the home courtyard of my father.

At least not the one outside of Bethlehem.

You see,
it was somewhere on that journey
that I heard
another divine whisper,
one that would change my course,
one that said:
"From this day forward,
until far beyond the end of time,
you will be a shepherd of people,
guiding all those who have lost faith in themselves,
others, and God
and lead them home to God's fold of forgiveness."

So, for some two thousand years
I've shepherded people
—who, by the way,
are generally a hell of a lot smarter
than any sheep I've ever known—
people like you
on the only road that leads you home to yourself,
God and community,
confession road,
telling, as we travel,
some of my stories
about truth and forgiveness
and listening to some of your stories about sin.

You know,
it's amazing how far a story can take you.

In fact,
I believe
stories can carry you all the way to salvation

because when you tell a story about your sins and sufferings
they become a lot easier to bear.

So, let me tell you a story
I like to tell everyone
who plods along confession road.

It's an old story about the truth.

One warm day
the truth was walking along confession road
seeking someone to guide
when he came upon a beautiful lake.

Invited by the cool water to take a swim
the truth stripped off his clothes,
hung them on a bush,
and jumped in.

Well,
while truth floated freely in the water
falsehood came walking along the same road
seeking someone to lead astray.

Upon seeing truth's clothes hanging on a bush
falsehood had an idea.

Falsehood stripped off his own clothes,
hung them on the bush,
put on truth's clothes and stole away.

Eventually
truth came out of the water
and discovered that
falsehood had switched clothing with him.

Truth, however,
refused to put on falsehood's clothing,
which is why we refer to him today
as the naked truth.

Truth is creation's first born,
born of honesty and self-esteem
while falsehood is fashioned out of fear and denial.

If honesty is the best policy,
as so many of you like to proclaim,
then I just don't understand
why you don't purchase a little insurance.

The premium isn't that high.

It costs only the price of truth
and that's usually pretty fair.

On confession road
only the truth can help you
strip off the rags of falsehood,
help you honestly face your actual sins,
help you admit that you are perfectly imperfect,
and help you open the closets
where your secrets hang wrapped in shame.

Now,
while I know
that not every secret you keep closeted away
is a sin,
I also know
that every sin wants to remain secret.

That's why on confession road
you must travel with the naked truth,
you must be honest with yourself
before you can walk honestly with others and God.

Now,
as I said earlier,
I tell this story about the naked truth
to everyone I shepherd on the road,
usually with very positive results.

However,
let me tell you about one rather anxious traveler
who seemed confused about the meaning of God's forgiveness.

The man listened intently to my truthful tale
as we walked together,

paused momentarily,
and then much to my surprise
responded angrily.

"I've been telling the truth
ever since I started the journey on confession road,"
he said.
"I've stood naked before God,
admitted over and over how I've hurt other people,
broken the covenant with community and God,
missed the mark,
committed what I shouldn't have
and omitted to do what I should have.

"I've done my part, shepherd,"
he yelled,
"I'm waiting for God to do God's.
I'm waiting,"
he concluded,
"for God to forgive so that I can forget."

Without a moment's pause
I responded firmly to the traveler's flawed notion by telling him,
"You are sadly mistaken,
my friend,
if you think that God's forgiveness means your forgetness.

"After all,"
I asked,
"how can you learn from your mistakes
if you don't remember them
and then remember them and then
remember them again?"

To forget your sins
is to throw away dearly purchased experience.

The strongest people don't forget their weaknesses,
the most successful never forget their failures,
and the greatest saints don't forget their sins.

After all,
God's forgiveness
doesn't wipe away or erase your memory.

It does,
however,
give you permission to let go of the guilt.

Remembering is the only way to salvation.

Let me tell you another story
that might help clarify the confusion
some people have
about forgiveness and forgetness.

This is a story about forgiving others.

While walking one day on confession road
I listened to a woman
tell the tale of how she had been trapped
in a very destructive marriage.

The story she told of her husband's cruelty
was beyond belief,
but I listened
as she wove the details
of her marriage and divorce together.

Finally I asked,
"Have you forgiven your former husband?"
to which she quickly replied,
"No, I haven't.
I'm still," she said,
"consumed with hatred for him."

"In that case,"
I said,
"you're still trapped."

Now,
I know that there are some people
who believe

that you haven't truly forgiven someone until
you've forgotten how and when they hurt you.

That's nonsense!

Forgiving others
doesn't mean that you forget the harm they inflicted
but rather that you face, embrace
and then let go of your resentment.

Here's the choice.
You either embrace your anger or it will strangle you.

As a radical psychiatrist once said,

"The stupid neither forgive nor forget;
the naive forgive and forget;
the wise forgive (themselves and others)
but they do not forget." (Thomas Szasz)
They do,
however,
learn from the remembering.

After all,
if it's the truth that sets you free
then it's remembering that keeps you free.

Let me share a classic tale
that may help move you along
confession road.

The story is about a famous actor
who was invited to a party
where he was asked
to recite for the pleasure of the guests.

Having recited a few common verses,
the actor asked
if there was anything in particular
the gatherers wanted to hear.

After a few moments
an older priest asked to hear Psalm 23,

"The Lord Is My Shepherd."

The actor paused for a moment
and then said,
"I'm willing to recite it
but on one condition
—that you will recite it also,
after I have finished."

Well, the priest was taken by surprise.
"I'm not a famous actor,"
he said,
"but, if you wish,
I'll recite it too."

The actor began quite impressively.
His voice was trained
and his intonation was perfect.
The audience was spellbound
and when he finished there was great applause.

Now it was the old priest's turn to recite the same psalm.

His voice was not remarkable,
his tone was not faultless,
but when he finished
there wasn't a dry eye in the room.

The actor then rose and with a quavering voice said,
"Ladies and gentlemen,
I reached your eyes and your ears,
but this priest has reached your hearts.

"The difference is this:
I know the Psalm but he knows the Shepherd."

My friends,
if you know the Shepherd
you know the way home to forgiveness.

Shhhhhhh.
Can you hear it?

Listen!

We must be close to home now
because I can hear divine whisperings.

Oh,
you may hear the whisperings of God
in different languages;

In Polish you may hear "PRZEBACZENEI."
In Italian, "PERDONO."
In German, "VERZEIHEN."
In Japanese, "YURUSU."
In Swedish, "FORLATA."
In Spanish, "PERDONAR."
In Gaelic, "MATHANAS."
The message, however, remains the same:
forgiveness.

Since God is a given,
for giving,
it's God's task to shepherd you along confession road,
whispering all the while,

"Welcome home.
Welcome home."

THE
ROCK THROWER

JOHN 8:2-7

At daybreak
Jesus appeared in the temple again.
All the people came to hear him,
and he sat down and began to teach them.

Then the teachers of the law
and the Pharisees
brought in a woman
who had been caught in the act of adultery.

They made her stand in front of everyone.
"Master,"
they said,
"this woman has been caught in the act of adultery.

"Now the law of Moses
orders that such women be stoned to death;
but you,
what do you say?"
They said this to test Jesus,
so that they could have some charge against him.

Jesus bent down
and started writing on the ground with his finger.
And as they continued to ask him,
he straightened up and said to them,
"Let the one among you who has no sin
be the first to throw a stone at her."

THE ROCK THROWER

I just stood there in the temple,
leaning against a pillar
in the Court of Women,
tossing a rock up and down in my hand,
trying to decide
whether or not I should throw it
at the adulterous woman
whom the simple-minded teacher,
Jesus, was trying to protect.

I knew
that when the scribes and Pharisees
dragged this criminal before the teacher,
demanding that he pass the prescribed punishment,
he would revert to type,
handing out forgiveness instead of judgment
—some of that sentimental love for enemies
he'd been preaching about all morning—
instead of the heavy hand of the law.

What this Galilean taught
was heresy against the status quo,
destructive of proper social order.

This Jesus wasn't
just another foolish preacher.
His message was dangerous.

After all,
this woman deserved punishment for her crime.

She was one of them.
She was an adulteress.
God, she was one of them!

The older penalty of strangulation
would've made a better example of the woman,
but stoning would have to do.

At least,
I was ready to dispense the proper judgment.

It wasn't,
however,
until this Jesus said,
"Let the one without sin cast the first stone,"
that my arm flew into the air with a resentful rage.

Life hadn't been fair to me
so why should I be fair?

Life had kicked me around enough
to teach me only how to kick back.

Cruelty tightened my grip around the rock
as years of bitterness stretched the muscles
of my shoulder
so that the stone
would fly with vengeful aim.

Anger lifted my arm high in the air
as self-righteousness took control.

Suddenly,
in the split second
just before I would set the rock free
to do its damage,
there appeared in my awareness
a revealed imaging.

Instead of seeing the adulteress woman
standing before the teacher and the crowd,
I saw myself,
with my flaws,
my arrogance and my anger.

Suddenly,
I realized that
I was one of them,
a weak human being.

When I turned back
to look at the rock
I held so high and mightily
in my hand,
I saw my name etched on its rough surface.

That's when I learned
the lesson that the teacher
had been preaching in the temple that day.

In that instant of revelation,
I saw that I and the woman were one.

We were kin in sin and forgiveness,
connected by something thicker than blood,
by the spirit of our frail humanity.

If I condemned her,
I damned myself.

If I deprived her of dignity,
I lost my humanity.

Remorse ran up the muscles of my arm
while humility lowered it to my side.

When I looked around the courtyard
to see if anyone had seen my violent act,
I discovered
that everyone else had quietly slipped away.

I was the last to shamefully leave,
carrying the weight of my arrogance
as I moved toward the door.

I wanted so much
to say something to the teacher
before I left,
perhaps even
to beg for forgiveness from the woman.

Instead,

I silently slumped against a pillar in self-disgust.

It was then
that I heard
the courageously compassionate teacher
say to the woman,
"Neither do I condemn you. Go and sin no more."

Even though
it has been years since
I heard Jesus speak
those words of forgiveness and challenge
in the temple courtyard,
I still remember them.

I hope he meant them for me, as well.
I also
still have the rock
I picked up that day in the temple,
and, yes,
it still has my name
etched on its rough surface.

LAZARUS

JOHN 11:41–44

Jesus lifted up his eyes and said,
"Father, I thank you, for you have heard me.
I know that you hear me always;
but my prayer was for the sake of these people,
that they may believe that you sent me."

When Jesus had said this,
he cried out in a loud voice,
"Lazarus, come out!"

The dead man came out,
his hands and feet
bound with linen strips
and his face wrapped in a cloth.

So Jesus said to them,
"Untie him and let him go."

LAZARUS

First
let me thank you for
inviting me to rise up out of death
to speak through your imagination.

It's indeed an honor
to speak on behalf
of the guestimated seventy-four billion people
who've died since the beginning of history,
give or take a few million.

For those of you wondering who I am
let me introduce myself.

My name is Lazarus
and I've done this rising from the dead thing before.

The reason I come to speak with you during this rising,
however,
is quite different
than when Jesus called me forth from the tomb
many years ago.

Basically,
I'm here to remind you
that although we,
the deceased,
have physically died
we still live on.

Oh, we may have been radically changed by death
but as long as God lives everything lives.

After all,
all there is is aliveness.

At this point,
I imagine you'd probably like me to explain

exactly what life after life is like.

Well that's a problem,
because even if I did describe it
you still wouldn't understand.

Trying to describe the after-life
reminds me of the old story
of the student who asked his teacher
to describe the moon.

The wise teacher,
in response to the student's question,
simply pointed at the moon.

The student,
of course,
thought he understood,
so he ran around telling all his friends
that the moon looked just like a finger.

If I told you what the after-life was like,
you'd probably run around
talking about
heaven, hell, purgatory, golden gates and harp-playing angels.

You'll just have to take it on faith
that life is not ended with death
but is rather dramatically changed.

Therefore,
because we,
the deceased,
do live on after death,
I'm here to protest
on behalf of the inalienable and legitimate rights
that are due us in justice,
to proclaim a bill of rights for the deceased.

First,
we have the right to be remembered.

Memory, after all,
makes the dead come to life
in an effective way.

The only way you can hug the dead
is through memory.

When you,
the living on this side of the grave,
remember us,
the living on the other side of the grave,
by writing our names in a book of memorial.
By etching on a concrete and marble wall
the 50,000 names of the Vietnam War dead,
by sewing a patch for the AIDS quilt
or by visiting our graves on a day of anniversary,
you bring us to life
in your imaginations, hearts and memories.

When you remember us by name
you light the flame of life for us.

Now,
when I say that we,
the deceased,
have the right to be remembered,
I do not mean,
however,
that you should cling to the dead.

Quite the opposite.

Clinging in grief
to someone who has died
will not bring you or them to life.

There's a story we often tell in the after-death
to illustrate the difference
between remembering and clinging.

The story is about a deceased young girl
and her father's grief.

When the daughter joined us beyond the grave,
we gave her
what we give every newly deceased person,
a candle to light the way on her eternal journey.

The father's grief was so ferocious,
however,
that his tears keep snuffing out the flame
that would guide his daughter on her way.

It was only after we sent a dream
into the father's sleep
that he finally grasped the paradox
that if he and his daughter were to have life,
and have it to the full,
he had to first let his daughter go.

The second right of those who have died
flows from the first.

Not only do we,
the deceased,
have the right to be remembered,
but we have the right to be remembered as we truly were,
not merely as you wish we had been.

Whitewashing our lives
by recalling only the pleasant memories
does those of us who have died
a great injustice.

To truly honor our memories,
you must recall our light and darkness,
our successes and failures,
our beautiful and painful struggles.

Remember that the full life we lived
belongs to us
as much as our names did.

To ignore our pain,
mistakes and struggles

is to deny what made us most human.

Oh, it may make you feel better
to forget
that your father was an alcoholic
or that your wife had been abusive
or that your son lived wrapped in anger,
but in the final analysis
denial only takes life,
it does not make life.

Remembering the whole truth about those who have died,
and not just
what makes you feel comfortable,
is the only way
to set you and us free
to continue the journey
of life and eternal life.

The next right due in justice
to those of us who have died
is the right to be prayed to and prayed for.

At any time you choose,
you can touch us through God.

Since we are where God is,
you can gather strength for your journey
or share strength with us
for our journey by simply praying,
by placing yourself
humbly in the presence of God.

As life does not end with death,
so neither does the love
shared between human beings.

In fact,
it could be said
that it is only through love
that we come to life

and live eternally.

A love relationship,
established in the life-before-death
can continue to grow in the life-after-death.

Love never dies.

It can only continue to make life.

There is no better way
of loving those of us who have died
than by holding our names in your hearts
so that God can see them there
and do what God does best,
love us into fuller and fuller aliveness.

Loved ones travel best,
after all,
when they are bound by the kinship of prayer.

All we ask
is that you pray
that we who have died
might know the more-and-more of God's love.

If you do that,
we promise to share that love with you.

The last right
due those of us
who have passed beyond death
is the right to be judged by God alone.

Did you know
that what most people believe
about life-after-death is true,
that in the final analysis
you get what you deserve?

The way I like to put it is
that you ultimately get what you've given.

Actually,
it's not really necessary for God to judge
those who die
because we pass judgment on our ourselves.

What you get in the after-death
is what you've given in the before-death.

Let me tell you a story
about what happened one day
while I worked as keeper of the gate
to the after-life to illustrate
just how human beings
pass judgment on themselves.

There was a wealthy man who died
and came before me
as gatekeeper to eternal life.

"Can I help you?"
I asked the rich man.

"I hope so,"
he replied.

"I'd like to enter paradise,
but I can't seem to open the gates."

"I'm sorry, sir,"
I answered,
"but I can't help you."
"Well, who can?"
the wealthy man demanded.

"It's quite simple,"
I responded.
"All you need
is the testimony
of someone to speak on your behalf,
and the gates will swing wide open.

"Did you bring anyone with you
whose witness

might help you open the gates?"
I asked.

"I certainly have,"
answered the man.

"I've brought the pastor of my church,
to which,
by the way,
I contributed generously.

"Oh,
I may not have given quite ten percent of my income
to the church
—it was a fairly well-to-do church anyway—
and although
I didn't go to church very often,
I still gave quite a bit of money over the years.

"I'm sure my pastor's testimony will open the gates."

"I'm sorry,"
I replied,
"but the witness of your pastor
won't open the gates to new life.

"Did you bring anyone else to speak on your behalf?"
I asked.

"Yes I have,"
the rich man answered
"I've brought my wife and children.

"Certainly
their testimony of my love for them
will be enough to open the gates.

"Oh,
I may not have been the best husband or father
in the world,
and I know
I didn't spend the kind of time with them
that I should have,

but I'm sure
they will tell you themselves
that I showed my love by being a good provider.

"I worked hard
all my married life
to keep my family
in the comfortable style
to which they had grown accustomed.

"I expect the testimony of my family
will do the trick
and open the gates."

"I'm sorry, sir,"
I answered.
"This is not a trick
and your family's witness to your work addiction
will not help you open the gates either.
Have you brought anyone else
to testify on your behalf?"
I asked again.

"Of course I have,"
he answered angrily.
"I've brought all the people
I served along the way.
You see,
before my death
I was the publisher
of many fine books in psychology, philosophy and religion.
In fact, my publishing house
published some of the best-selling
self-help books on the market.
The books not only made my company a great profit,
but they helped quite a few people as well.
I'm sure
the gates of paradise
will open
once the testimony is heard

from all those I've helped."

"Again,"
I was required to say,
"I'm sorry to inform you,
sir,
but the witness of those you made a profit from
won't help open the gates either."

"Well,
whom else was I supposed to bring
to help me open the gates,
for God's sake?"
the wealthy man yelled.

"God,"
I replied.
"Didn't you bring God with you?"

My friends,
we the after-living
ask only what is due us in justice
—the right to be remembered,
the right to be remembered as we truly were
not as you wish we had been,
the right to be prayed for
and prayed to
and the right to be judged by God alone.

One last story,
however,
before I let your imaginations go.

It's a story
about a young man
who sincerely doubted
the existence of the after-life.

One night,
while sleeping under the stars
the young man dreamed
that he was face to face with God.

The doubtful young man
finally had the chance to ask God,
"Is there or is there not life after life?"

God thought about the question for a moment
and then said,
"Hey,
if human beings can make plastic,
don't you think God can create eternal life?"

THE
HAUNTED PRIEST

LUKE 10:30-31

Jesus then said,
"There was a man going down
from Jerusalem to Jericho,
and he fell into the hands of robbers.

"They stripped him,
beat him,
and went off leaving him half-dead.

"It happened
that a priest was going along that road,
and saw the man,
but passed by on the other side."

THE HAUNTED PRIEST

First,
let me thank you
for the opportunity to tell my side of the story.

Of course,
it has been almost two thousand years now,
so my memory may be a bit hazy.

As I remember it,
however,
it was on Yom Kippur.

That's right!
It was on the Day of Atonement.

Anyway,
while I was waiting in a huge crowd of pilgrims
outside the temple of Jerusalem
for the priests to process out with the ritual goat,
I spotted a man I thought I recognized
standing not ten feet away from me.

O my God,
I thought.

Could this be the same man I had seen
lying half-dead in a ditch
on the Jericho road only a few months earlier?

Could this be the man I'd passed by?

My first instinct was to do exactly what I did
the day I saw the man lying in that ditch.

I wanted to run.

What if he recognized me?
I thought.

But then again,

perhaps I was just seeing things.

I'd been fasting and praying in repentance all day,
so perhaps my hunger was causing me to hallucinate.

This stranger couldn't be the same man.

No one could have survived such a beating.

I shifted to see past the people standing in front of me
—yes, it was he.

As I recovered from the shock
of seeing this ghostly memory come to life,
I wondered if I should say something to the stranger.

Perhaps,
I thought,
I should tell him how often I had prayed for him,
or, at least,
try to explain why I didn't stop to help.

Perhaps he'd understand my predicament at the time,
how difficult a decision it was to pass him by.

Perhaps he'd even be compassionate enough to forgive me.

Now I know that there are a lot of people
who have already jumped to the judgmental conclusion
that only someone cruel and arrogant
could ignore a man so desperately in need.

Just another typical priest.
Right?
Thinks he's better than others.
Right?

It's not that simple and you know it.

Let me tell you
why I was traveling the dangerous Jericho road.
Perhaps then you'll understand.

You see,
my family is of the priestly class,

a proud and loyal lineage in Israel.

Anyway,
when the lot was drawn
deciding which clan would serve for a week in the temple,
my family name was chosen.

Of course,
as the eldest son
I was obligated to fulfill my duty
to family, temple and nation.

Don't you see?
I had waited years to represent my family at worship.

I might never get the chance again.

I couldn't just throw away
one of the most important opportunities of my life
to pick a dying man's carcass
off the side of the road.

If I had touched that man
or let him touch me,
I'd have become unclean,
requiring the ritual purification,
during which time I wouldn't be allowed to serve in the temple.

That's the letter of the law.

I was torn. My choice was between two goods.

Either I performed my duty
in the name of family, tradition and institution
by worshipping in the temple,
or I fulfilled my obligation to charity
by giving comfort and aid to a fellow traveler.

Now, I wasn't stupid.

Like every other Jew,
I'd been taught when I was young
that religion
is greater than the sum of its laws and rituals,

that right and wrong
are best built on the foundation of justice,
and that what ultimately matters
is how you have loved.

Still, I passed the beaten man by.

It wasn't fair.

Why, I wondered,
should I be the one required to stop and help this man?

It wasn't my fault that he'd been beaten down.
Why should it be my responsibility to pick him up?

After all,
I was about the business of worship.

I don't know where this stranger was going,
but it certainly wasn't to fulfill temple duty.

Anyway, he got what he deserved,
traveling alone on the Jericho road.

Didn't he know how dangerous the journey could be?

I certainly did—

which is, by the way,
another reason why I didn't stop to help the man.

What if the thieves and robbers
who had beaten this foolish traveler
were waiting behind the rocks for another victim?

I'd be easy prey for the pickings.

It was just too dangerous.

I did exactly what fear told me to do.
I ran like hell.

Now don't look at me like that,
as though you would have done anything different.

Just then,
while still waiting in the anxious crowd outside the temple,

my attention shifted again—
this time,
from the man I had passed by on the road,
to the high priest
who had returned to the altar
in the holy of holies for the third time.

Because I knew that this was the moment
when the high priest would lay his hands on a goat
and make confession for the people and nation,
transferring our sins onto the animal,
I bowed my head.

That's when I remembered something a young rabbi had said
while teaching in the Court of Women
earlier that day.

"Repent and believe in the good news,"
he proclaimed.

"Repentance,"
he continued,
"begins when you take responsibility
for the wrongs you've committed
or the rights you've omitted.

"After all," the rabbi said,
"running away from yesterday's
mistakes, fears or poor decisions
is like trying to run away from your feet."

Suddenly the crowd pushed forward.

I looked up to see what was happening
only to find myself
looking directly into the eyes of the man
I had passed by on the road.

As we stood staring into each other's hearts,
I hardly even noticed
as the temple priests processed by with the ritual scapegoat,
leading it out into the desert
to throw off a cliff.

DANIEL OF
EMMAUS

LUKE 24:13–32 (PARAPHRASED)

On the third day,
two disciples,
Cleopas and a companion,
were going to Emmaus,
a village seven miles from Jerusalem.

As they traveled
they talked about the things
that had occurred in the city
during the previous three days:
how Jesus the Nazarene
was handed over by the priests and rulers
to be crucified,
how some had hoped that he would be the one
to redeem Israel,
and how others had claimed
that he was risen from the dead.

It happened
that while they were talking and wondering,
Jesus came up and walked with them,
but their eyes were prevented from recognizing him.

DANIEL OF EMMAUS

Hello.

My name is Daniel of Emmaus,
and although
I know you've never heard of me,
I'm pretty sure you've
heard the name
of one of my oldest and dearest friends,
Cleopas of Emmaus.

Let me start from the beginning.

Cleopas and I have known each other
all of our lives.

In fact, the midwife
who brought me into the world
birthed Cleopas
only a few months later.

We've been practically inseparable ever since.

We played together as children,
worked in the fields together as boys,
stood for each other at our weddings,
prayed together in our little village synagogue
and cared for each other's families
as if they were our own.

Cleopas and I were friends.
We trusted one another.

That is precisely why
I decided to tag along,
when Cleopas announced
on a rainy spring day
that he was going on a Passover pilgrimage
to the city of Jerusalem
to meet the preacher

Jesus of Nazareth
and to break bread with the holy man.

Jesus was all Cleopas
had talked about for almost two years.

He would quote Jesus' parables.

He would tell Jesus' miracle stories.

Why,
Cleopas even kept a written record
of some of the tales
he heard about Jesus
from pilgrims passing through our village.

I certainly couldn't refuse
when Cleopas asked me
to accompany him
on the half-day journey
to the great city
so that he could fulfill his dream
of seeing and eating with the Christ,
especially after he had heard rumors
that Jesus had recently
been paraded through the streets in triumph.

Of course,
the crowd of pilgrims
that descended on the city
for the Passover feast
didn't make the search for Jesus very easy.

In fact,
it seemed that no matter
where we searched,
whether within
or outside the city gates,
we were caught in tides of traffic.

For example,
when we heard that Jesus

was going to be teaching in the temple courtyard,
we rushed there as fast as we could,
only to discover,
after fighting our way through the crowds,
that Jesus had already moved on.

Even when we stood
in a long line of pilgrims
waiting to sacrifice our unblemished lamb,
thinking that we might catch sight
of Jesus doing the same,
we were disappointed.

No matter how hard we searched
Jesus seemed to stay
just one step ahead of us.

We missed him in the Court of Women
when he preached there.

We missed him in the Court of the Gentiles
during the sacrifice of the lambs.

Why,
we even missed Jesus' appearance
in the Gethsemane garden,
and that's after we were given
secret information that
he could be found praying there
immediately after the Passover meal.

Of course,
by the time
Cleopas and I arrived,
Jesus had already been arrested
and was on his way to be condemned.

Although
despairing at the possibility
that Jesus would be hung out to dry,
Cleopas and I
still waited to catch a glimpse.

We were there when the soldiers
publicly scourged Jesus,
dragged him through the city streets
and crucified him on Golgatha hill.

Only then
did we finally get close enough,
just close enough to see Jesus die.

After all our expectations and dreams,
what we ended up seeing
was a godly man
die an inhuman death,
being taken down from a cross,
being wrapped and anointed by his followers
and then being laid in a garden tomb.

In the face of such
disappointment
all Cleopas and I could do
was return home
to our families,
to our work,
to our prayer,
to our waiting.

Of course,
we heard the strange story
from a woman we met
as we made our way
out of the city
that Jesus had supposedly risen from the dead.

We thought
the rumors of his rising
were greatly exaggerated.

The fantasy did little to raise our spirits.

After all, we had come all the way to Jerusalem
to break bread with a living Jesus,
not to stare into the face of death.

Of course,
once on the road returning home to Emmaus
Cleopas and I
did what lifelong friends tend to do
when disappointed by life.

We shared what we felt
as we watched Jesus being nailed to a cross,
as we watched hope being buried beneath human cruelty.

We didn't have to use a lot of words
to communicate a lot of feelings.

All we had to do
was look into each other's eyes
to see the confusion and hurt
buried there.

Our broken bits of conversation and silence
would carry us down the dusty road
to the village we knew so well.

Suddenly, however,
as Cleopas and I
took a final turn home,
a shadow fell over us.

From out of nowhere,
the strangest of strangers
was walking directly behind us.

Cleopas and I turned quickly around
to face the stranger.

Cloaked from head to toe,
to protect himself
from the heat and dust of the day,
the stranger startled us again
by asking if he could
accompany us on our journey.

Aware that the Emmaus road
could be dangerous

if traveled alone,
we welcomed the man.

The company,
I thought, might even be a healthy distraction
from the sadness of the city,
until, of course,
the stranger asked Cleopas
what we had been discussing along the way.

Cleopas,
being an honest soul,
immediately began telling the stranger
about the crucified teacher.

Cleopas even took out his book
of quotes, stories and parables,
and for the next few hours,
while we wandered at a snail's pace,
they argued with so much animation
that you'd think Cleopas and the stranger
were rewriting the commandments.

Although the journey
from Jerusalem to Emmaus
was only a half day's walk
I found myself awfully weary
when my companions and I
finally shuffled into the still village
late in the evening.

While I, however, was tired,
Cleopas seemed changed by the miles.

With a firmness I'd rarely
heard in my friend's voice,
Cleopas spoke up.

"We will share a meal at my home tonight."

As Cleopas put
a jug of wine and a loaf of bread

on the familiar family table,
it was my turn to speak up.

"Cleopas," I said,
"I'm sorry you weren't able
to see the face of the living lord
and to share a meal with him."

"Oh, but I have," Cleopas answered.
"I certainly have.
Don't you see Daniel," he said
"that the face of God
is the face behind all others."

Turning slowly on Cleopas' comment
I realized that there were no strangers
sitting at the table,
only companions breaking bread.

THE
WINE STEWARD

JOHN 2:1-12

Three days later
there was a wedding at Cana in Galilee
and the mother of Jesus was there.

Jesus was also invited
to the wedding with his disciples.

When all the wine
provided for the celebration
had been served
and they had run out of wine,
the mother of Jesus said to him,
"They have no wine."

Jesus replied,
"Woman, your thoughts are not mine!
My hour has not yet come."

However,
his mother said to the servants,
"Do whatever he tells you."

Nearby were six stone water jars
meant for the ritual washing
as practiced by the Jews;
each jar could hold twenty or thirty gallons.

Jesus said to the servants,
"Fill the jars with water."

And they filled them to the brim.

Then Jesus said,
"Now draw some out and take it to the steward."

So they did.

The steward tasted the water that had become wine,
without knowing from where it had come;
for only the servants who had drawn the water knew.

So, he immediately called the bridegroom to tell him,
"Everyone serves the best wine first,
and when people have drunk enough,
he serves that which is ordinary.

"You instead
have kept the best wine until the end."

This miraculous sign was the first,
and Jesus performed it at Cana in Galilee.

THE WINE STEWARD

My name is Samuel of Nazareth
and I'm possessed by the blood of the grape.

To put it in more contemporary terms,
I'm what you'd call a recovering alcoholic.

Now,
although I've been sober
one day at a time for almost two thousand years,
I still get pretty nervous
when I'm asked to tell my story,
so forgive me if I ramble a bit.

Perhaps it would be helpful
if I began by
doing a little archeology around my drinking.

As a Jew
who grew up during the biblical period of history,
I was accustomed to drinking wine.

It was part of the Jewish lifestyle.
When we got sick,
we drank wine as medicine.

When we socialized or celebrated,
we drank to mark the occasion.

And when we were depressed,
we drank to escape.

Wine was our cup of joy and sorrow.

In fact,
we even drank when we worshipped.

For example, on every sabbath
as we raised a cup of the grape,
we prayed the Kiddush prayer;

"The seventh day
is consecrated to the Lord our God.

"With wine,
our symbol of joy,
we celebrate this day and its holiness.

"We give thanks for all our blessings,
for life and health,
for work and rest,
for home and love and friendship,
on the sabbath,
eternal sign of creation.

"We remember
that we are created in the divine image.

"We,
therefore,
raise the cup in thanksgiving.

"Blessed are you,
Lord, our God,
king of the universe,
who creates the fruit of the vine."

Now,
I know it was rather rare,
during biblical times
for a Jew to addictively drink to excess,
especially since we were weaned
on the juice of the fermented grape.

I, however,
was such a rarity.

It was my only claim to fame.

I had heard the admonition from the book of Proverbs:
"Wine is reckless, liquor rowdy.
Unwise is anyone whom it seduces" (Proverbs 20:1).
I had heard it preached a million times.

Preaching, however,
never stopped me from drinking.

In fact,
now that I think about it,
I can't remember a time in my life
when I wasn't poisoned by the venom of the grape.

Why,
the fermented demon
even manipulated me into becoming a wine salesman.

Any excuse to be around the juice of the vine
was a good enough reason for me.

I even drank with the Romans,
the very enemies of my people.

They were some of my best customers.
I wasn't a bigot.
I drank with anyone.

Sad to say but wine became my best friend.

Actually,
it would be more accurate to say that
wine became my only friend.

I knew for the longest time that I was sick.
My life had become chaotically unmanageable.

I just didn't know what I could do about it.

Actually,
I had no life to speak of,
at least not until I stopped drinking.

I remember the day I had my last drink.
In fact, it was the last time I got drunk.

You see,
I couldn't just have one drink.

I was an all-or-nothing kind of guy.

If I drank I got drunk.

That is exactly what happened
at the wedding banquet
of a family friend in Cana of Galilee.

You see,
even though I had volunteered
to function as the wine steward for the wedding—
just to make sure that the wine flowed freely
and that everyone had a good time—
I still proceeded to get roaring drunk.

In fact,
I was so soaked in the grape
that most of what happened at the wedding
is just a blur.

I remember traveling the nine miles
from Nazareth to Cana,
with my sister Mary,
of course,
slipping out of sight
every now and then
to have a quick drink.

I remember arriving at the home of the groom's parents,
leaving Mary to help tend to the food preparations
for the banquet
and then
making my way to the wine market
to purchase the many jars of wine needed
for the days of wedding celebration.

I remember standing with a fellow wine merchant
inspecting some wine,
raising a cup,
and then…and then…

The next thing I remember I was
dancing with,
of all people,

my nephew,
Jesus of Nazareth.

Now,
for the overly pious among you,
I don't mean that Jesus and I were spiritually dancing.

We were at a Jewish wedding,
and like good Jews,
we were dancing up a storm.

Of course,
at the slightest hint of a storm,
Jesus would stretch out his hands to try and calm it.

Certainly a different man, that Jesus!
Some even called him strange.

Now, I hadn't seen Jesus for almost a year
before he appeared at the Cana wedding
with some of his disciples,
but as soon as he arrived
at the reception,
the whispering started.

"Is he or isn't he a prophet?"
some asked,
while others dared to blaspheme,
wondering if Jesus was actually the long-awaited Savior.

He was my nephew.

I had seen him wet his diapers.

The chances of Jesus being the highest power,
the messiah,
were about as high as the chances
that he could change water into wine,
or, even more impossible,
convince me to stop drinking.

Obviously,
I had no idea who he was from the inside out.

I must tell you, though,
that he was an unusual boy
who became an uncommon adult.

He never picked up his father's carpentry trade.
He spent almost all his time reading the Torah
or talking with the rabbis.

He was a dreamer,
a storyteller,
a naive boy whose head was stuck in the clouds.

What was even more embarrassing
to the family,
however,
was that when Jesus moved from Nazareth
to the sea town of Capernaum,
he took up
with the likes of fishermen and tax collectors.

God,
the boy had no shame!

Now that I think of it, though
I do remember my sister Mary
introducing me to one of Jesus' followers
at the wedding party.

His name was Simon Peter,
and from the smell of the man,
it wasn't hard to guess his profession.

You may not believe it,
but this fisherman tried to argue with me,
a grape trader,
about how long you could store new wine in old skins
before they burst.

The fisherman had rocks in his head.

Not as big,
of course,
as the rocks in the head of the groom at the wedding.

Now, there was a fool.
And don't you think I didn't tell him so
before I stormed out of the reception.

Imagine, hiding six large jars of the finest wine
from your own wine steward
and then acting as though nothing had happened.

I mean,
who was he to save the best wine until last
without telling me!

It made me look like an idiot
in front of the guests.

It made me look as if I couldn't do my job.

Of course, I was drunk—
so drunk
that I had no idea what happened to me
after I left the party.

That's when I must have passed out.
God, what a drunk!

I don't remember
being picked up by Jesus and Simon Peter,
nor do I recall camping with them
for the night
along the Capernaum road just outside of Cana.

But that's what must have happened,
because when I woke up hours later,
I found myself only a few yards from a warm fire
with Peter's loud voice echoing in my ears.

Well, I just lay there.

I just lay there by the fire
for the longest time,
embarrassed to open my eyes,
listening to Peter tell Jesus a story
about a gossiping servant.

Now,
the way Peter tells it,
it seems that
a servant at the wedding
had started a rumor
that after Jesus had learned
that I hadn't purchased
enough wine for the party,
he, as casually as you please,
changed one hundred and twenty gallons of purification water
into the best tasting wine in all of Cana.

Peter laughed uproariously at the telling of the tale,
concluding his story with a strange statement:

"Always looking for the magic, these people,
while missing the miracle and the meaning."

A number of odd thoughts crossed my mind
after hearing Peter's tall tale.

First, I wondered
if Jesus had been
as surprised as everyone else
by the magic he had performed at the wedding.

And, second,
I wanted to learn how to do it.

Just imagine,
I could be a drunk able to turn water into wine.

To tell you the truth,
I felt miserable as I lay there in the dirt.

I knew I was a loser,
a drunk,
possessed, fixated, obsessed,
insane for the escape the grape could provide.

However, drinking just wasn't any fun anymore.

All drinking did was cause problems.

I couldn't even do my job right.

I wanted to stop.

I just didn't know how.

God,
it felt as if I had a God-sized hole
in the middle of my head, heart and spirit,
and all I could do
was try to fill it with whatever felt good
—wine, powdered potions, women, whatever.

Lying there with my eyes tightly closed,
I wanted to scream:

"If there is a God, show yourself.

"God, I surrender.

"I give up.

"I'll do anything if you'll
just fill up my emptiness."

Finally,
after lying in the dirt
for as long as I could take it
I slowly cracked open my eyes.

Sitting directly in front of me
was my nephew Jesus.

As the light from the fire danced on his face
it slowly dawned on me
that perhaps the real miracle of the Cana wedding
wasn't so much
that Jesus could change water into wine
but rather that he could change me.

THE VINEDRESSER

LUKE 13:6–9

*And Jesus continued with this story
about a man who had a fig tree
growing in his vineyard,
and he came looking for the fruit on it,
but found none.*

*Then he said to the vinedresser:
"Look here,
for three years now
I've been looking for figs on this tree
and have found none.*

*"Cut it down!
Why should it use up the ground?"*

*The gardener replied to him:
"Leave it one more year,
so that I may dig around
and put in some fertilizer;
and perhaps
it will bear fruit from now on.*

*"But if it doesn't,
you can cut it down."*

THE VINEDRESSER

Did you know that
some of the stories Jesus told
actually occurred
on one of the largest
wheat, grape, olive and fig farms
in all of Capernaum,
where, by the way,
I happened to be the head vinedresser,
the master gardener?

The farm was huge,
running from the flatlands
along the Sea of Galilee,
where we planted wheat and barley,
right up into the hills,
where our vines and fruit trees
grew strong.

It was a four hundred-acre farm
that I lovingly call my backyard.

You see,
I was born,
grew up
and worked on that farm
preparing for the day
when my father
would pass down to me
the job of vinedresser,
just as his father
had handed down the job to him.

(You could say,
if you dared such an awful pun,
that I became the plant manager.)

As my father always said,

"Next to family and faith,
life's greatest treasure is the land."

Of course,
I know you're not here
to listen to my life story,
so let me tell you
where I first met Jesus.

Actually, our first meeting
wasn't a very dramatic event.

In fact,
it was quite ordinary.

You see,
very early each morning,
during the seasons of planting and harvesting,
I'd go into the city of Capernaum
to hire the number of laborers
needed to work
in the fields or vineyards that day.

That's right.
I was Jesus' boss.

Of course,
little did I know the day I spotted
the tall lanky Jew from Nazareth,
standing with all the other common day laborers
waiting to be hired,
that in the next few years
Jesus would become my right-hand man on the farm,
and then, of all things,
he would quit the land,
be baptized in the Jordan River,
start a healing ministry
in and around Capernaum,
have followers of his own,
and eventually be
crucified on a cross.

How Jesus could have gotten himself
into so much trouble is beyond me.

He never struck me as someone
capable of the blasphemy and insurrection
that the religious leaders and politicians
accused him of.

He certainly was a hard worker,
though.

I can vouch for that.

In fact,
I was so impressed
with Jesus' spirited energy
and his popularity among his fellow workers
that after only one season of day work,
I hired him to be my full-time assistant.

Of course,
I could never promise
Jesus the position of vinedresser.

I had two sons preparing for that task.

Naturally,
like my father,
I planned on handing down my job
to one of my sons.

They really were good boys
once you got to know them.

And boy, they were strong.

Hey, they took after their father, right?

Of course
the boys went through
some of those growing stages
that every parent likes to complain about.

The worst phase by far, however,

was when they would say one thing
and then do another.

It drove their mother and me crazy.

For example,
every morning
I'd send my sons
out into the fields
so that they could
learn the trade of vinedressing.

Of course,
it was common for the older boy
to say
that he was going out into the fields to work
and, then,
to stay home,
while it was just as common
for the younger boy
to absolutely refuse
to put his hands to the plow or planting
and, then,
go out and work like a mule anyway.

Jesus, however, was a different story altogether.

He was consistent and persistent,
a man of his word.

However,
he was never meant to be a vinedresser.

Jesus just had
too much of the storyteller in him.

For example,
no matter what work we were doing together,
Jesus would be in the middle of telling a story,
and more often than not,
it was a story
he had already told me at least ten times.

Of course,
I didn't have the heart to tell him
that he was being repetitious.

I just couldn't take away
the obvious enjoyment he felt
in the telling of the tales.

He certainly loved a good story.

In fact,
I must have heard Jesus say,
at least a thousand times,
especially when talking with my sons,
that the only thing
that can live as long as the land
is a good story.

And God,
could he tell them!

For example,
when Jesus would spin the tale
about his father's death,
I felt as if I was right there with him,
wondering how he was going to support his mother
and, then, being surprised when he found a job
clearing rocks on a farm
just outside the village of Nazareth.

As I said,
he certainly could
go on and on with the tales.

For example,
Jesus would tell the story
about a young man who
took his share of his inheritance,
left home,
was beaten up on the road,
was saved by,

of all people,
a Samaritan,
and, then, returned home
not only to discover his father's love
but also to unearth the treasures of life
buried in his own backyard.

No sooner would he finish telling that story
than he'd started telling it again,
with,
of course,
a few new twists or turns
thrown in for good measure.

Jesus was a great storyteller.

I never imagined,
though,
that he'd eventually
story himself onto a cross.

I guess he was just too honest
for his own good.

Too generous with his effort.
Too trusting.

Really,
just too naive.

Jesus had faith, though.
I've got to give him that.
God did have faith.

When, for example,
the master of the farm ordered
the sowing of seed for the planting,
Jesus took him at his word
and sowed with such an enthusiastic spirit
that I had to step in to make sure
that some of the seed actually fell
in the plowed field.

And when the master
hired day laborers
to help in the harvest
and then paid
them equal wages
no matter how many hours they worked that day,
Jesus didn't complain
like some of the
other day workers
or threaten to riot
like some of the tenant farmers.

Jesus,
you see,
had faith in the master's judgment—
at times, it seems,
a good deal more faith than I did,
and I was the master's vinedresser.

I can't remember
a more faithful
or hard-working man
than Jesus.

Why,
he even had a small garden of his own
that he'd tend late in the day
after returning from the fields.

It was odd,
though,
that Jesus sowed only mustard seeds
in his own garden.

He said something about
trying to solve the mystery
of why the smallest of seeds,
which when ground to powder
made a very potent spice,
would grow,

when planted,
into one of the strongest and largest of trees.

In fact
as a master gardener
I can testify
that whether cultivated or growing wild
mustard trees are almost
impossible to kill.

They are like,
say,
a fig tree—
which reminds me of a story
about a fig tree
that really strained Jesus' faith
in the master.

"How can the master
be so cruel?" Jesus ranted.

"Couldn't he give it another chance?"
Jesus raved,
after I told him that the master
wanted us to cut down
a diseased fig tree
growing on the edge of the orchard,
before it infected
the entire vineyard.

Of course,
I told Jesus
that for three seasons
I had tried everything I knew
to heal the tree,
but that didn't stop him
from asking
for more fertilizer
and one more chance.

So I gave him permission to care for it.

With that Jesus wasted no time.

Jesus picked up his sleeping mat,
moved up to the orchard,
lit a fire for the night,
offered a prayer,
and, then,
at first light
set to work
to answer his own prayer.

He fertilized
with just the right mixture of
manure and dirt
so as not to shock the tree.

He pruned
some of the tree's larger branches
so that the roots wouldn't have to work so hard,
and he told the tree
one story after another
about other barren trees
that had recovered
to produce again.

Of course,
Jesus knew that
there is imperfection and weakness
in every vineyard,
that there are weeds growing
in every wheat field,
and that you can't force a tree
to produce fruit
if it chooses not to
or if it's sick beyond repair.

After all,
Jesus knew he couldn't cure the tree.

All he could do was care for the tree
the best way he knew how

by giving it
the opportunity, the ingredients
and the encouragement it needed
to cure itself.

Sadly,
though,
after many trying weeks,
Jesus finally realized
that the fig tree
would never rise or recover,
that it would never produce fruit again,
that it was dead—
unlike,
of course,
the story about the fig tree,
which, as you've just heard,
still lives on.

As does the sacred storyteller.

THE
MONEY-CHANGER

JOHN 2:13-16

As the Passover of the Jews was at hand,
Jesus went up to Jerusalem.

In the temple court
he found merchants selling oxen, sheep and doves,
and money-changers
seated at their tables.

Making a whip of cords,
he drove them all out
of the temple court,
together with the oxen and sheep.

He knocked over the tables
of the money-changers,
scattering the coins,
and ordered the people selling doves,
"Take all this away
and stop turning my Father's house
into a marketplace!"

THE MONEY-CHANGER

Having finally learned that
it's better to tell the truth
than to own it,
that it's better to be honest
than merely right,
I've decided today to make
an uncommonly honest confession.

Now,
don't throw anything at me
when I tell you,
but I was a banker
in the city of Jerusalem
during the reign of Herod
and the rise and demise of Jesus of Nazareth.

Not only
was I a banker,
but I was the temple money-changer
who spread the maliciously false story around
that Jesus,
after preaching a revolutionary sermon
in the temple court
condemning the corruption and commercialization
of the temple grounds,
had not only violently lost control of himself
but had viciously attacked me
and many other good, loyal
and hard-working money-changers,
with a whip.

To tell you the truth,
my version of the story
was a bit exaggerated.

Actually I lied.

Oh,
Jesus did argue with me
and a few other merchants and money-changers
in the temple court that day,
and the table of coins
did get knocked over in the midst of discussion,
but, as far as
the rest of the story is concerned,
well,
Jesus didn't really
try to hurt anyone.

Who would have thought
that my version
of the temple ruckus
would make it into print?

I mean,
how could anyone fall
for such a tall tale?

Wasn't it obvious, if Jesus had
actually tried to start a riot,
as I originally claimed,
that he would have been arrested
by the Roman guards
for disturbing the peace?

I never meant to hurt the man.

But damn,
I was mad—
angrier
than I had ever been in my life.

You see,
I just couldn't understand
how this Jesus could march right into the Court of Women
and preach against
those of us
who worked for the temple.

Didn't this wild-eyed reformer
have any respect for those of us
who made an honest living
by helping others worship
according to prescribed custom?

After all,
it wasn't my fault
that the priests and Pharisees
decided that no coins bearing the face of a false God
could be used to purchase
the required doves or sheep
for temple sacrifice,
and that only shekels could be used,
thus requiring some of us
to function as official money-changers,
for a small profit,
of course.

It wasn't my fault
that the temple administrators
opened the courts
to merchants and bankers alike
and then taxed us
on our measly profits.

I just couldn't understand
why this Jesus
was preaching against me.

I thought we had
an understanding.

You see,
I knew Jesus.

Well,
to tell you the truth,
I really didn't know him that well.

Actually,

I had one brief conversation
with him,
in a crowd of pilgrims,
just outside the city gates
a few days before Passover.

I felt a bit awkward at the time
just standing there next to him.

Of course,
I didn't really know what to say,
so I stammered on a bit,
and then asked him about...
asked him...
what did I ask him...?
Oh yes,
now I remember.

I asked Jesus
what I had to do
to gain everlasting life.

Good question, right?

Well,
I was a bit taken back
when he not only answered my question
but then proceeded to challenge me
to give what I had to the poor and to follow him.

I smiled at his recommendation,
gave him a little donation,
and moved on.

I never expected
that Jesus would
not only appear in the temple court
a few days later
but would go out of his way
to embarrass me and my fellow bankers
by accusing us of putting

money before God and family,
comfort before compassion
and compromise before concern
for the poor.

God, was I angry,
and, as I realized later,
a little scared—
scared because I knew he was right.

I confess,
I was a greedy man.

I loved money.
There, I said it.

God, I loved money.

For me,
shekels not only counted,
they ruled.

In fact,
no matter how many times
my father had told me
when I was young
that there was
a time for everything under heaven
—you know—
a time for love, a time for war,
a time for work, a time for sleep
etc., etc.,
I just couldn't imagine
when it wasn't
the right time to make money.

Why,
I had piled up storehouses of grain,
pens of sheep and oxen
and treasuries of shekels
as though it was all manure,

which,
as you know,
may help things grow when spread around,
but, when piled high,
God,
it stinks as though there's no tomorrow.

Now, I know the manure image
may be a bit disgusting,
but that's exactly
how I felt,
as if I was covered
with sh...shame
for being so greedy.

Of course,
if the manure image
is a bit upsetting,
think of me as a fat camel
weighted down
with so much in the way of
greed, possessions,
desires and fears
that I couldn't
fit through the gate
of respectability in this life
or the next.

I guess
the real reason I was angry at Jesus,
though,
wasn't so much because
he did or didn't
turn the money-changers'
tables upside down
—that's almost irrelevant—
but rather
I was angry because Jesus' preaching
turned my heart,

my values,
right side up again.

You see,
for years
I had worked like a mule,
promoting, protecting
and making a profit
from the status quo.

In fact,
I put so much confidence
in the temple institution
that I had practically
lost my faith
in God, myself and others
in the bargain.

I spent so much time marching around,
proclaiming from the rooftops
my great belief
in the institution of the family,
that I had practically destroyed my relationship
with my wife, my children,
with the very people
I claimed to love.

What a hypocrite!

I paid alms tax for the poor,
all right,
but you can bet that
I never went near or touched
anyone who was poor.

I may have been a successful
business and community leader,
but I was becoming a lousy human being.

I was rich
but,

God,
was I hungry!

I was wealthy
but empty.

Of course,
I wasn't always so obsessed
with filling up my
storehouses with grain,
my pens with sheep
and my temple holdings with shekels.

There was a time when
I knew that
no matter how you rationalize, analyze,
theologize, politicize or compromise,
that no matter how
you slice, dice or price it,
that no matter how hard you pretended
or how hard you worked
to get what you've got,
it has never been,
it will never be
nor is it now
right
that some people
have too much
while others don't have enough,
that some have luxuries
while others lack necessities.

It's simply not right.

Now,
for those of you still listening,
let me give you a warning.

This Jesus is a dangerous man.

In fact,

he's so dangerous
that he can turn your life
upside down if you're not careful.

God, is he dangerous!

In fact,
I promise you,
if you let this Jesus
preach in your churches, synagogues,
temples or meeting houses,
there's no telling
what might happen.

Why,
you might even be transformed
by his challenging words.

THE
PRODIGAL'S FRIEND

LUKE 15:20-24

The son was still a long way off
when his father caught sight of him.

His father was
so deeply moved with compassion
that he ran out to meet him,
threw his arms around his neck
and kissed him.

The son said:
"Father,
I have sinned against God and before you.
I no longer deserve
to be called your son."

But the father turned to his servants:
"Quick!
Bring out the finest robe
and put it on him.
Put a ring on his finger
and sandals on his feet.
Take the fatted calf and kill it.
We will celebrate and have a feast,
for this son of mine was dead
and has come back to life.
He was lost and is found."

And the celebration began.

THE PRODIGAL'S FRIEND

Come!
Join the celebration!
You're all invited!
Come on!
Follow me!
Everyone's invited!

The prodigal son has returned,
and his parents are having
a welcome-home feast.

The fatted calf has been killed.
There will be food on the table,
and wine in the jugs.
There will be music, singing and dancing.

As a lifelong friend of the family
and in the name of the prodigal's
mother and father,
I invite you to come and celebrate,
for their son was lost and is found,
was dead and has come back to life.

You're all invited,
so come to the feast.

Who's going to be at the celebration?
you wonder.

Well,
the widow's going to be there.

You know,
the crazy old widow from the village
who's always either losing her money
or giving her last shekel to the temple.

She'll be there.

The widow wouldn't have a problem
about going to a party
to welcome home a prodigal.

Of course,
that's probably because
she can't remember what the boy did wrong,
anyway.

She remembers
how to have fun, though,
so the widow will be there.

And
the master of the neighboring farm—
he'll be there too.

You know the landowner I'm talking about—
the one who pays equal wages
to his day laborers
no matter how many hours they worked.

He wouldn't miss this feast for the world.

And, of course,
the prodigal's father and mother
will be there.

Now,
the father,
well,
he'll be dancing with joy,
sort of making up for all the time
he spent out on the road
waiting for his son's return,
wishing all the while he had been a better father.

It was sad to watch,
but on almost every sabbath,
the father would be at synagogue,
with his oldest boy on his right
and an empty seat on his left.

He'd put his head in his hands
and he'd pray.

Actually,
I think,
he was crying.

The father wept a lot while he waited.
And he wondered,
if he could have done anything
to prevent his younger son
from taking and wasting
his part of the family's inheritance.

Perhaps
he should have given his younger son more attention,
he thought,
or maybe
he shouldn't have given him so much freedom.

Well,
all a father can do is
love the best way he knows how.

Of course,
while the father danced his son's sins away
the boy's mother,
with a heart torn by love,
had the little prodigal pinned to the wall
so she could get a full confession.

She wasn't about to let her younger son
practically break his father's heart
without hearing the whole sordid story.

No beating around the (burning) bush with her.

As you can see,
everybody who isn't anybody
will be at the celebration.

Of course,

there are some neighbors and family members
who have already excused themselves
from the party,
for rather lame reasons, too.

For example,
one local farmer
said he just bought five oxen
and had to stay home to take care of them.

And,
of course,
as for the prodigal's older brother,
well,
he won't be at the celebration either,
so you don't have to worry
about him spoiling your fun.

He's still so angry
that his father
doesn't love him more
than he loves his younger brother
that he's off pouting somewhere.

And, naturally,
since the older brother won't be there
well,
neither will be any of his
so-called friends.

It's all for the best,
though.

At least
you won't have to listen to their
whining and moaning.

"Why should I go to a party
for someone who shamed his father?"
one said to me.

"He should be punished for his sins,"

another said,
"not welcomed home with a feast."

"Or,"
as another complained,
"you just watch—
that prodigal will do it again.

"After all,
once a disappointment,
once a failure,
once a loser,
once a sinner,
once a disgrace,
once a thief, liar, addict,
always a...
well,
you know.

"You can't change
a camel's smell,"
he concluded.

You're in luck,
though.

Not only won't you have to put up with these self-righteous fools,
but there's plenty of room for you at the feast.

Because the father and mother
love their son,
they've sent me out onto the highways and byways
to invite you to come to the feast.

It doesn't matter where you've wandered in life,
you're still invited.

Whether you're poor or rich,
more or less broken,
crippled, lost, blind, sinful,
addicted or lame,
come to the feast.

Come and celebrate.

Be a friend of the father's
by befriending the son.

Come and celebrate
in favor of the forgiveness
found in friendship and family.

Come and celebrate
the kind of friendship
that doesn't just overlook faults and failings
but rather chooses to look right through them
to that something divine
that lasts many times longer
than any mistakes or sins—hope.

Come and celebrate
the kind of family
where you spend your time
caring for one another
rather than trying to change one another.

Come and celebrate
the kind of friendship
that appreciates
how far you've come
rather than demands to know
how far you've got to go to be perfect.

Come and celebrate
the kind of family
that understands how much courage it takes
to make a mistake and admit it,
and how much harder it is to return home
the longer you've been away.

Come and celebrate
with a feast full of friends and family.

Come and return home to yourself.

THE
CROSSMAKER

MATTHEW 27:22–23

Pilate said to the crowd,
"And what shall I do with Jesus called the Christ?"

All answered,
"Crucify him!"

Pilate insisted,
"What evil has he done?"

But they shouted louder,
"Crucify him!"

THE CROSSMAKER

My name isn't important.

All you need know is
that I was a crossmaker.

Along with many other carpenters
in the city of Jerusalem,
I was pressed into the service
of carving the crossbeams
used for crucifixion by the brutish Romans.

What could I do?
I had to feed my family.
I knew how the Romans used these beams
but I couldn't do anything to prevent it.

So,
almost every morning
I'd go into the hills
to cut down
strong pieces of timber
to drag home for the carving.

Once chiseled,
I'd pile them high in the Romans' courtyard.
I despised the job,
but the money put food on the table.

After all,
how these crossbeams were used
was not my concern.

My first obligation was
to take care of my wife and children,
not to ask questions.

Oh,
when I think back

on the days of my apprenticeship,
when I first took up the trade of a carpenter,
I can recall
the joy I felt
when carving a table
from coarse pieces of heavy wood.

I've always thought myself a skilled carpenter—
not the best,
perhaps,
but one in love with the craft.

It's an art,
you know, to mold and fashion
from rough beams
a smooth and well-fitted piece of furniture.

It takes an eye of care
and hands of compassion.

This may sound strange
to those of you
who do not know the feel of wood,
but to be a true carpenter
you must respect the grain and bend
of each and every beam you cut
or it will not fit well.

I sound like a dreamer,
and I was,
so many years ago.

Then reality hit
with the cruelty of a world gone mad.

My ideals seemed to fall away
like the bark of a dying tree.

With each problem and setback in life,
I became more and more pessimistic.

Even the love of my craft

seemed to slowly crack
into splinters of callous indifference.

My art became a tool of death,
my craft a means of suffering,
and I didn't seem to care.

My friends,
it's one thing to say,
"I didn't know,"
when finding fault with your actions.

It's another thing entirely
to know your actions
contribute to the heavy burdens
others must carry
and to say,
"I don't care."

Not knowing is ignorance
and can be understood;
not caring
is the very evil
Christ came to overcome.

You may wonder
why I've come to speak with you today.

Well,
I, Christ's crossmaker,
watched this holy man
carry upon his shoulders
what I had chiseled with indifference
and hewed with fear,
and I became sick with shame.

I beg you,
therefore,
my friends,
to watch the suffering Jesus
of today's crucifixion

walk the steps of the passion
as innocent children go hungry
and the helpless are oppressed
by bureaucratic idiocy.

Watch Jesus nailed to the cross
of today's violence
as the powerless are victimized
by weapons of holocaust,
built out of fear.

Watch closely
as Christ carries his cross today
and ask yourself
if,
by your silent indifference,
you've helped to carve that cross.

If so,
put down your chisel of abuse,
for I guarantee you,
no one carves a cross
for another to shoulder
without one day
having to carry it himself.